Denise Wymore & Jim Jerving

The 2020
VISION OF MARKETING

A Focus on Purpose

ISBN: 1450515487
ISBN-13: 9781450515481

PART ONE

THE 2020 VISION
OF MARKETING

Chapter One

Introduction

How do we systematically go about forgetting everything we know, before it destroys us?

—Tom Peters

We're experiencing the worst economy since the Great Depression; there is a faint light at the end of the tunnel if you're an optimist, if you are a pessimist there is darkness. Marketing professionals are being laid off, budgets slashed, sponsorships dropped, newspapers folding, and a general malaise is washing over the world of advertising.

Pepsi decided to forego advertising during the 2010 Super Bowl, ending its 23 year run. According to the ESPN blog[1] PepsiCo Inc. spent $33 million in advertising during the 2009 Super Bowl, but in 2010 shifted dollars to a new marketing effort that is mostly online rather than focusing on a single event. The cost for a 30-second spot for the Colts versus Saints at the Super Bowl was $2.6 million. And that was just to air it; that didn't include the cost to make it.

Remember the Pepsi challenge? The blind taste tests between Coke and Pepsi? That was traditional marketing; obsessed with winning in their category by pushing me-too products. We know; we just made Coke and Pepsi drinkers angry. We're not their target audience, we don't like cola, and when we taste them, there's little difference. The reason

---

1 http://sports.espn.go.com/nfl/news/story?id=4751415

we have passionate Coke and Pepsi drinkers is because of the reputation. Awareness and history—that's a brand.

In 2010, Pepsi invested in social media. That doesn't mean they are creating a Facebook fan page. Instead, they are allotting $20 million for a "Pepsi Refresh" project. People can submit their ideas online to help their community and Pepsi drinkers vote on the projects. Their goal is to create positive word-of-mouth. What has this got to do with soft drinks? Absolutely nothing. *The word "marketing" should be italicized*

Steve Jobs released the iPad in 2010. Observers are skeptical. Why? Because there is nothing else like it. Adults are cynical creatures. We are more comfortable with a new thought, idea or product if it can be related to something we already know. This iPad is not really a laptop, or a hand-held DVD player, or a video game, or a book, yet it could make all of these things obsolete.

Jobs has shown us two things: 1) Organizations don't have values, people do, and 2) When you truly understand what business you are in and use that knowledge as a filter to question everything, you can't lose. *That's the 2020 vision of marketing.*

Jeff Bezos, CEO of Amazon.com, predicts that this book you are reading will never be printed on dead trees. If you're reading this in paperback, it's because Amazon.com also owns the print-on-demand company that published this book. Today the majority of his profits still come from the printed form, but he is planning on, and in a real sense creating, a future where the printed word is obsolete. Bezos is the master of spreadsheet-defying logic. *That's the 2020 vision of marketing.*

Satmetrix, the Net Promoter Company, released their 2010 Industry Benchmarks for insurance, financial services, airlines, telecommunications, technology and online services industries. It's no surprise that Apple and Amazon.com are the leaders in their industries.

"A company's ability to deliver a superior customer experience relative to its industry peers is a critical indicator of customer retention and new customer acquisition through positive word of mouth," said John Abraham, general manager of Net Promoter programs at Satmetrix. Traditional marketing is no longer the catalyst for growth—reputation and word-of-mouth are. *That's the 2020 vision of marketing.*

We should've seen all of this coming. Just ten years ago, in preparation for what was to be the end of the world as we know it—Y2K—marketing took a reputation beating. Quite simply, when preparing for mass hysteria, collapse of the economy and martial law, marketing was labeled a non-essential function.

This should've been a warning shot. The label implied frivolity to some degree. In a crisis, we cease all marketing efforts. It begs two questions: What is the real purpose of marketing? And can we live without it forever?

Well, you know how that story ends. January 1, 2000, came and went without a bump. Marketing resumed—business as usual. We didn't get to find out.

In this book, we hope to lay the groundwork for the 2020 vision of marketing. We believe with all of our hearts that if we continue to rely solely on campaigns, bribes, brochures and newsletters to grow our business we are toast. We also give credence to the notion that the future CEO must not emerge from a finance background, but rather from sales and marketing. The CFO's job is to count the beans; the CEO's job is to develop strong, lasting relationships with the customer to drive sales revenue. *That's the 2020 vision of marketing.*

Marketing in the next ten years must make a dramatic shift from quarterly focus to long-term viability. That means we abandon ROI on direct mail for the discipline of measuring reputation. We need to look beyond the newsletter articles promoting products to enabling communication with our customers through social media tools. The harsh reality becomes one of relevance. Are the marketers today equipped with the *relevant* talent and skills to become communicators, rather than stalkers?

Marketers will need new skills as technology makes it possible to interact directly with customers, collecting and mining information about them and tailoring their products and services based on that data, according to the authors of "Reinventing Marketing," in the *Harvard Business Review*. But no amount of technology can improve an organization's efforts as long as marketing departments are set up to market products rather than cultivate customers:

"Companies must shift their focus from driving transactions to maximizing customer lifetime value. That means making products and brands subservient to long-term customer relationships. And that means changing strategy and structure across the organization—and reinventing the marketing department altogether."[2]

---

2 Rust, Roland; Moorman, Christine; and Bhalla, Gaurav. "Rethinking Marketing," Harvard Business Review, January-February, 2010.

Chapter Two

The CEO as Pilot

Organizations don't have values, people do.

Today we are looking to blame some *thing* or some *one* for our economy. Blaming Wall Street bankers, of course, is easy. After all, it was the most visible culprit in the collapse of the mortgage industry and resulting unemployment, foreclosures, bankruptcy and the Great Recession.

The political party that you're not affiliated with is also guilty. One could argue that Republicans got us into this mess, and Democrats are prolonging it. An argument that will never be won, but it's fun to debate. And while we're talking about it, let's discuss capitalism—the ultimate definition of greed, according to some viewpoints. Surely those values are to blame for our economy's collapse.

Time Magazine recently published their own list of the "25 People to Blame for the Financial Crisis: The Good Intentions, Bad Managers and Greed behind the Meltdown." Number 5 on the list: American Consumers—you and me. Economics is the study of human behavior. And if the economy is in crisis, then we have been behaving badly. As William Shakespeare wrote in *Julius Caesar* more than 350 years ago:

The fault, dear Brutus, is not in our stars, but in ourselves...

The job of an economist is similar to a meteorologist or astrologer. It's a guessing game and you're allowed to be wrong—frequently. Why is this? Because humans behave, like the atmosphere and the celestial bodies, randomly and are ever changing, mysterious and fickle.

We offer this opinion on our current economic condition: The economy fails because our society's values fails. We are all to blame. When a company fails, the CEO has failed. That's why they get the big bucks. Because organizations do not have values, people do. And the person at the top of that organizational chart is piloting the plane in a direction based on their own personal, fickle, ever changing, sometimes random, deeply held values. If you're an employee, you are along for the ride. If you're a marketer, you should be in the cockpit with the CEO, as co-pilot.

The Pilot of the Economy

Alan Greenspan was the longest serving Fed Chairman in U.S. history, from 1987 to 2006. Some blame him for the mortgage crisis by allowing banks to become increasingly deregulated. *Time Magazine* ranked him Number 3 on its list of guilty parties.

During congressional hearings, Rep. Henry Waxman D-California, chairman of the Oversight and Government Reform Committee, asked Alan Greenspan if he felt he had made mistakes in his policies as chairman:

Greenspan: *I made a mistake in presuming that the self interest of organizations, specifically banks, and others, was such that they were best capable of protecting their own shareholders and their equity in the firms.*

It's been my experience having worked for 10 years at a major international bank, that loan officers of those institutions knew far more about the risks involved to the people to whom they lend money than I saw even our best regulators at the Fed capable of doing. So the problem here is something which looked to be a very solid edifice and indeed a critical pillar to market competition and free markets did break down and I think that shocked me. I still do not fully understand why it happened.

Waxman: *Did your ideology push you to make decisions that you wish you had not made?*

Greenspan: *Ideology is a conceptual framework with the way people deal with reality, everyone has one. You have to. To exist you need an ideology. The question is, whether it is accurate or not. Yes, I found a flaw, I don't know how significant or permanent it is, but I've been very distressed by that fact. The flaw in the model that I perceived is the critical functioning structure that defines how the world works, so to speak.*

Greenspan is saying that his flaw was in trusting human beings not to be greedy. Greenspan's ideology is that free competitive markets are by far the unrivaled way to organize economies. We tried regulation, none meaningfully worked.

The values of the Federal Reserve chairman led to lax regulation because he had faith that CEOs would operate in the best interests of their shareholders. He trusted bank CEOs, executives, boards, the rating agencies and others in the financial services industry to do the right thing. They didn't.

Whether you're aware of it or not, the way you make decisions, big ones or small ones, involves a filter. And this filter is created from your life's experience or your values. In business, part of this filter should be your brand, which is influenced by your values, but more strategic in its directive. Singer songwriter Bob Dylan puts it best: *A man hears what he wants to hear and disregards the rest.*

Here's another example: Bonnie Hammer, CEO of USA Network, uses her brand filter to help determine which shows are aired. Her team asks a routine set of three questions about each possible show:

1. Does the show have a fun sensibility?
2. Does it have a "blue sky" tone of hopefulness?
3. Does it revolve around an "aspiration," if quirky, a lead character with a moral and ethical center?

If the answer is affirmative to all three criteria, the show will be aired on the "Characters are Welcome" USA Network. And it supports their values.

Shows like "Monk," "Wings," "Burn Notice," and "NCIS" easily pass through this filter. Shows like "Jersey Shore," "Survivor," and anything with Simon Cowell have trouble passing through the filter.

Chapter Three

Bottom Line Filter

Can you imagine a pilot of a plane, on a cross-country flight, scanning the financials of the airline rather than concentrating on navigational instruments? Not terribly concerned with where they are going as long as they are still making money. Short-sighted behavior could lead to a fiery death.

How does a person take a 103-year-old venerable financial institution and create the largest bank failure in US history? It's really important for the CEO of 2020 to understand their role. If your only filter for making decisions is the bottom line, you'll fail.

Kerry K. Killinger joined Washington Mutual in 1982 when it acquired a brokerage firm, Murphy Favre. He became president in 1988, was named CEO in 1990, and became chairman in 1991. Washington Mutual was a fairly small player in Puget Sound. Through a series of acquisitions, Killinger built up a large West Coast presence. Known for their completely free checking and quirky ads, customers hijacked the branding and named it WaMu. Soon branches were popping up all over the map, more like a Starbucks than a bank. WaMu had a stellar reputation.

Then things changed. Killinger decided WaMu would aggressively pursue mortgages—specifically the subprime market. The culture of WaMu for over 100 years was pursuing the American Dream. That dream was to own a home, not have a mortgage. WaMu began offering adjustable rate mortgages—interest only—pick-a-payment loans in areas where mortgages had been reserved for the upper middle class, like California and Florida.

Soon almost anyone with a pulse could get a mortgage with WaMu. Incentives drove loan officers to make "liar loans." Real estate agents partnered with WaMu to rake in record profits. Mortgage brokers were given handsome commissions for selling the riskiest loans with their higher fees, bolstering profits and, ultimately, the compensation of Kerry Killinger.

On September 8, 2008, the board of directors removed Killinger as CEO, but it was too late to fix the bank's problems. The damage had been done and just 17 days later, on the same day Washington Mutual was chartered in 1889, WaMu failed on September 25. It was the largest bank failure in United States history. Who's to blame? The CEO—not Wall Street, not Bush or Obama—Kerry K. Killinger killed Washington Mutual.

Lessons Learned

Dare we say it? We admired Killinger for his business model. Because he had the right focus and executed it brilliantly. So what went wrong? It's simple: His values shifted from growth to greed.

To illustrate the impact of values shifting, or as Greenspan would call it, ideology and your company's reputation, we've developed a diagram called the "Ripple Effect" shown in Figure A. At the center are the CEO's values. These are not the ones framed on the wall in the board room. You must look to the second ripple to really see what is valued—culture. That is what is measured, managed and rewarded.

Figure A
The Ripple Effect

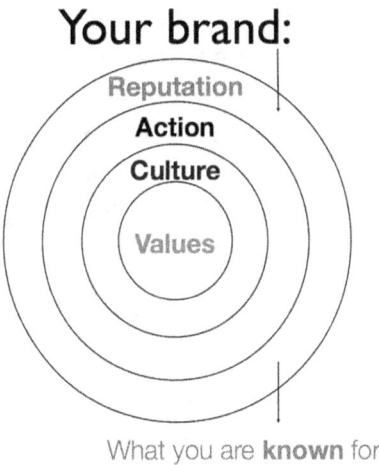

Your brand:

Reputation
Action
Culture
Values

What you are **known** for.

Peter Drucker said, "What gets measured gets managed." If you say you value service but reward risky loan approvals, you really value volume. You can preach the customer is king all you want but if you are holding people's feet to the fire on delinquencies, you are promoting a paranoid culture where the customer becomes the enemy. That's not to say that you ignore fraud, or risk, but rather balance those measures with brand-like measures.

Brand is your reputation. If you have a bad one, no amount of marketing is going to help you. The ripple effect of the CEO's values changing is a drastic change in reputation, or brand.

Reputation is the word on the street. It's all that matters today. What doesn't matter is what you think your reputation is. Perception is reality. If the customer perceives it—it's true.

That's a hard pill to swallow and why we think so few organizations allow the voice of the customer into the organization. More on that later.

The demise of the WaMu brand began in 2001 when the *American Banker* named Killinger Banker of the Year. In 2003, Killinger predicted that by 2008, Washington Mutual would not be identified as a bank. He said "We hope to do to this industry what Wal-Mart did to theirs, Starbucks did to theirs, Costco did to theirs and Lowe's and Home Depot did to their industry."

Killinger had a major impact on the banking industry, but it wasn't the type of effect that he had in mind. Killinger decided to focus on building a reputation around free checking; many credit unionists still believe that the checking account is the primary financial institution indicator. His goal was to offer totally free checking and to cast shame and doubt on his competitors. And he did it well.

Then, to show his commitment to the American Dream, he shed the car loan business. We know this from a friend who had a checking account with WaMu for eight years and needed a new car loan. Because he considered WaMu to be his primary financial institution, naturally he went to his branch. The response was, "We no longer do car loans, but when you and your wife need a home loan, we can beat anyone."

From a marketing perspective WaMu ran brilliant ads. That began in the Pacific Northwest with the rodeo grandmas. Wells Fargo was coming across the border. Pacific Northwesterners are born and bred to hate Californians. The rodeo grandmas are real life women cattle wranglers from Ellensburg, Washington, all more than 60-years-old, who pledged to keep the West safe from checking charges.

This campaign put WaMu on the map and sent a clear signal to the rest of the United States that free checking means free checking. You have Killinger to thank for your inability to charge for this expensive service.

Once WaMu had a firm foothold in that business, it was time to crank up the mortgages. The Power of Yes! campaign made its debut during the 2003 Academy Awards. This was shortly after the acquisition of PNC Mortgage, Fleet Mortgage and Homeside Lending, making WaMu the third-largest mortgage lender in the United States. The Power of Yes! promoted loans to all consumers, particularly borrowers the other banks deemed too risky. And so began the downward spiral.

Money is a funny thing. When the measures and rewards changed at WaMu—the culture ripple—the action changed. Marketing supported the frenzy. We say "Yes" to almost everyone. According to a class action lawsuit filed by 90 employees, there was tremendous pressure to churn out bad loans. And this pressure came from the top.

While the mortgage side was booming, the retail side was also expanding. In 2000, WaMu introduced a unique branch design known as Occasio, which eliminated traditional teller windows and queues in favor of an open, circular floor plan. In 2004, it patented the design. This was Killinger's Starbucks vision—to create more of a conversational environment or gathering place. JP Morgan Chase, which purchased WaMu, returned the branches to traditional teller rows.

Some might say were it not for the mortgage bubble bursting in the sand states, WaMu would still be around. But here's the rub: Killinger, and many others, believed the bubble would never burst. That is delusional thinking that defies logic.

All market bubbles inevitably burst. One need only go back to the history books to the story of the tulip bulb bubble and collapse in Holland in 1637. Dutch farmers, weavers and speculators mortgaged everything they had to raise Guilders in a *Tulipomania* bid for bulbs. There was even a futures market for the bulbs and the price of tulip bulbs kept increasing until the bubble burst and bulbs were only worth a hundredth of their former prices.

Values, Filters and CEO Success Stories

If company failures result in CEOs being held accountable by losing their jobs, then successful companies should do the complete opposite, right? Well, in theory, yes. One of the greatest success stories—and almost failure—of our time is Apple. Today a 20-year-old might see Apple as an overnight success. Their first Walkman was the iPod with iTunes. Then they couldn't wait for Verizon to offer service on the 4G iPhone. Now that iPad is available, consumers will buy that instead of a computer.

What they don't remember was the historic advertising moment on January 22, 1984, during Super Bowl XVIII. Apple paid $1.5 million for 60 seconds. It drew a line in the sand, like WaMu's The Power of Yes! At the time, Apple Co-founder Steve Jobs' intent was to take on big blue, IBM.

Jobs made computers that were different than the big grey boxes. Interestingly, he chose not to compete with Microsoft. Even though he had a different operating system, he wanted people to see Apple as a choice. Being the biggest has never concerned him. Being the best was his obsession.

Today Apple still spends an inordinate amount of time and money on design. Design teams have to come up with ten options. Then those are narrowed down to three. More time is spent on three mockups. At the final stage, they nail down the best design of the three.

When the first iPod was being created Jobs' instruction to the designers was odd or intriguing depending upon your point of view.

"I want the buttons to look so good you'll want to lick them." The first iPod looked like an ice cream bar. Arctic white was the color. And its face was smooth and almost button-less. It was the polar opposite of hand-held electronics.

So where is Sony in the MP3 market? How did the inventor of portable, personal music devices not win the race for digital tunes? It all comes down to focus and this filter for making decisions.

Sony's downfall is its stubborn resistance to supporting the ubiquitous MP3 code in their early players. Many users found it frustrating to convert their MP3 music collection to ATRAC3 for use on the Network Walkman, while Apple's iPod supported MP3 out of the box and came with the superior iTunes software.

If your only filter is the bottom line—you'll lose.

Steve Jobs values filter has always been two words—user experience. It's his ideology and it has served him well.

In 1980, Apple launched the initial public offering of its stock, which generated more capital than any IPO since Ford Motor Company in 1956. Jobs and about 300 others became millionaires. In 1983, Apple launched the first personal computer to the public with a graphic user interface. It was a commercial failure, because it was too expensive. But that didn't discourage Jobs. His passion and his drive for perfection were undaunted ... and he continues to stay focused on that vision.

From 1985 to 1997, Jobs was no longer with Apple. He resigned after infighting and subsequently being relieved of his duties by CEO John Sculley. During that time he founded another computer company, NeXT Computer and Pixar. His user experience passion eventually created Academy Award-nominated films like "Toy Story." Today Jobs sits on Disney's board of directors. They share similar values.

Amazon.com and Bezos' Values

Jeff Bezos was a curious little kid who tried to dismantle his crib with a screwdriver. He graduated from Princeton with a computer science and electrical engineering degree. In 1994, while driving cross country from New York to Seattle he wrote the business plan for Amazon.com. He sold his first book out of his garage.

The name Amazon was chosen for a couple of reasons. First, it was named after the world's largest river. And when you searched for a company online—pre-Google days—the hits were listed in alphabetical order. The Amazon logo evolved with an arrow leading from A to Z, representing customer satisfaction—as it forms a smile—and the goal to have every product in the alphabet.

It's one thing to declare a vision, quite another to manage it and make it true. Bezos has been described as "a happy-go-lucky mogul and notorious micromanager."

Amazon.com was not the first online bookstore. Powell's in Portland, Oregon, was. Powell's bookstore was founded in 1971 and was famous for its sheer size. You receive a map when you walk through the doors. Rooms are color coded by category. It shelves new and used books side-by-side. It will buy your old books; the bookstore has an amazing coffee shop in the back where you can hang out. This was well before Starbucks came to town. It's a tourist attraction now. The difference between Powell's business model and Amazon's was quite clear. Powell's sells books.

Jeff Bezos didn't want to do that. Instead, his filter for building his business model was this: We make money when we help people make purchase decisions.

We went to www.powells.com recently. Its best seller book is *The Pacific* by Hugh Ambrose. There is a comment page, like a blog would have. And zero people have contributed. On www.amazon.com this book had nine comments two weeks after its release—an overall score of 2.5 stars out of a possible 5.0. One of the reviewer's comments, one that gave it the lowest rating, said this: *The best word to describe this book is tedious.* On the Powell's book site you can only read reviews that are placed there by the publisher, which is really marketing, not unbiased opinion.

The Pacific ranked number is 132 today on the bestsellers list for Amazon. As authors with books on that site we can tell you with certainty that the number ranking for sales changes hourly.

The list price is $26.95, and that's what you'll pay if you purchase it from Powell's. Amazon is selling it for $17.70 with free shipping for Amazon Prime members, or you can instantly download to your Kindle for $9.99.

Some would say Amazon is the Wal-Mart of booksellers. Sure, its prices are lower, but it also helps us make a purchase decision. There is no community at Powell's online. The physical store, however, is a great place to hang out and get lost in a good book. Powell's did nothing to differentiate itself online. If you don't know the brand, you won't get to know them on their website, because it just sells books. It's a lost opportunity in our opinion.

Chapter Four

Brand Filter & Target Audience

"Nike's goal is to inspire athletes all over the world. If you have a body, you are an athlete."

-Bill Bowerman, co-founder of Nike

When Nike co-founder Bill Bowerman made this observation many years ago, he was defining how he viewed the endless possibilities for human potential in sports. He set the tone and direction for a young company created in 1972, called Nike, and today those same words inspire a new generation of Nike employees.

Our goal is to carry on his legacy of innovative thinking, whether to develop products that help athletes of every level of ability reach their potential, or to create business opportunities that set Nike apart from the competition and provide value for our shareholders.

It started with a handshake between two visionary Oregonians—Bowerman and his University of Oregon runner Phil Knight. They and the people they hired evolved and grew the company that became Nike from a US-based footwear distributor to a global marketer of athletic footwear, apparel and equipment that is unrivaled in the world.

*Source: **http://www.nikebiz.com/company_overview/***

One of the most important discussions businesses need to have today is on the subject of target audience. Too often people confuse a territory or a broad demographic for a target.

If Bowerman says anyone with a body is an athlete; does that mean Nike targets every person on the planet? The answer is no. Name a brand that targets everyone? Some might say

Disney, Coke, and Wal-Mart. But they really don't. Just ask a Pepsi drinker.

Disney targets families with disposable income. It does not target single people. Have you taken a family of four to the Magic Kingdom lately? Just to pass through the entrance you're going to plop down several hundred dollars and then you have to buy the Mickey Mouse merchandise!

Disney does not target low-income families but Wal-Mart does. Anyone can shop at Wal-Mart, but not everyone wants to or needs to. Even when they tried to glam up the brand the reputation was still low-income.

If you read Nike's philosophy again, it target athletes— serious athletes. It will always be known for the quality of their running shoes. Nike was so obsessed with the weight of the shoes, Knight suggested it remove its trademark swoosh at one point. It was thought the lighter the shoe, the faster the runner.

The CEO's flight plan

Jeff Bezos and Steve Jobs not only share a strong passion and commitment, they also lead tirelessly from a vision that is summed up in their brand filters. Jobs took his filter and coupled it with a narrow target audience to create a differentiator in the music world that disrupted the entire industry.

Admittedly Apple was late to the game with his version of the MP3 player. Usually first to market has a distinct advantage. Nathan Schulhof, CEO and founder of Audio Highway, introduced the first MP3 player at the Consumer Electronics Show in January 1997. He is known as the father of the MP3 player industry. Never heard of him? This is because he made incremental improvements to durability and portability in music. He did not reinvent how we listen to our tunes.

Let us explain. Think back to your vinyl record album days. What was one of the biggest problems with vinyl? You couldn't play it in your car. The 8-track tape player was really created for that very reason. It was an increase in portability and durability. Not great, but it did the job.

Then along comes the cassette tape. The format was closer to what we were used to. We had Side A and Side B back. Eight tracks were confusing. It was difficult to find a song. Cassette tapes also brought us the magic of recording and with that, the birth of the mix tape.

One of our favorite movies is *High Fidelity* with John Cusack. He tells his story of love through the mix tapes. There's a scene in the film where he is sitting on the floor of his dumpy Chicago apartment surrounded by stacks and stacks of vinyl. Looking for just the right song to finish up his mix tape for a new girl he's met. That's dedication.

The compact disc (CD) was a giant leap forward for durability and sound quality. But the original format did not allow for recording. So, we were stuck replacing our vinyl on CDs and making cassette mix tapes. Sure, we bought an expensive CD changer. It had what was called a magazine feature. You could load up to ten CDs in this magazine and program your own playlist. This meant you were sitting on the floor surrounded by CD jewel cases, laboriously entering CD 3, song 12, and so on, song after song. It took hours depending on how long you wanted your party to last.

The original MP3 player played music. Most had a shuffle feature but none had the compilation tape makers dream that is iTunes. Steve Jobs relied on his values, vision and passion—user experience—combined with the psychographic target of the compilation tape maker to create iTunes. That is why the iPod dominates the MP3 player market.

A demographic target is too broad. Many believe that iPod targets younger people. Or that iPod targets everyone who likes music. Have you ever met someone that doesn't like music? Some form of music? The character Angela, on the sitcom "The Office" announced in an episode that she does not like music. That should give you some idea of the type of person she is.

Apple and iPod took a psychographic approach to defining the target for their entry into the music industry. Psychographic targets solve problems. And the problem that existed for mix tape makers was the ability to quickly and easily control and carry their entire collections.

How easy is it to make a mix tape on iTunes? It's insanely fast. We remember the first one made. We kept saying "You have to be kidding! This is it?" And our favorite feature, deleting for good those bad songs on all those albums we never want to hear again. Ones we had avoided by fast-forwarding or running across the room the lift up the arm on the record player and then gently set it down on the next track.

If you heard a great song on the radio, you had to write it down, wait for the album to drop, take the bus, and hope it was still in stock, buy it, bring it home and then pray that isn't the only good song on the album. One-hit wonders ripped us off.

Today I can be sitting in a bar, hear a song on the radio, hold my iPhone Shazam application up in the air, wait for the vibration, touch the screen and buy it. One song, one buck.

That's why music stores are gone. The iTunes is a disruptive technology.

According to the book *The Profit Zone*, there are ten strategic control points in business models. A strategic control point protects the profit stream that the business design has created against the corrosive effects of competition and customer power. The rapid growth of customer power in the past decade and a half has forced strategic control to the top of the priority list.

Every business design has at least one strategic control point. *The Profit Zone* was written before iTunes was launched. But it clearly illustrates why it's so successful. The highest profit-protecting power, according to authors Adrian Slywotzky and David J. Morrison, owns the standard. There sits Bill Gates and Microsoft's operating system and now Steve Jobs with his iTunes. Both have been sued over their dominance. It comes with the territory of being at the top of the heap.

But iTunes also protects its profits by having a strong brand. This is rated in the middle of the index. Right below that is the two-year product development lead.

Apple has always been the leader in innovation and constantly makes their products obsolete by creating a better one. Where Apple has never competed, and wouldn't dare is the bottom rung—commodity with cost disadvantage. This area of zero profit protecting power is reserved for the airline industry, General Motors and Bank of America. All too big to fail but they aren't too proud to take taxpayer money.

Solving Problems as a Marketing Strategy

There seems to be growing evidence that points to problem solving as not only a differentiator in the marketplace, but a silver bullet in terms of staying relevant. As we stated earlier, demographic targeting aims to appeal to a certain group of people. The psychographic approach solves a problem and the demographics become insignificant.

Consider Blockbuster, which was founded in 1985 to solve a problem. The economy was experiencing a recession, unemployment was up, interest rates were falling, and families had to tighten their belts.

Faith Popcorn, a trend forecaster and marketing consultant, coined the phrase "cocooning" in 1990. She identified this as a commercially significant trend that would lead to, among other things, stay-at-home electronic shopping. Blockbuster was capitalizing on this trend. In the early days the video renter also provided the video players and popcorn.

But Blockbuster got lazy. It created a problem that others were quick to solve. Having to drive to the store, to return the movie, or pay the dreaded "late fee."

Netflix was founded in 1997. Ten years later Netflix announced the billionth DVD delivery. Their original model was simple. Rather than driving to the store, we'll mail you the movie. Oh, and keep it as long as you want. We don't care. Blockbuster added a similar option, but it was too late. On September 23, 2010, Blockbuster filed for Chapter 11 bankruptcy protection.

Meanwhile, Netflix takes its model to the next level, offering instant viewing through—wait for it—another problem solver TiVo. Not only did TiVo solve the problem of annoying marketing, 90 percent of TiVo users no longer watch commercials, but added broadband features, including Netflix Watch Instantly.

The Kindle is quite simply a tree saver. If you have to move and are an avid reader, you dread packing up and hauling boxes and boxes of books you'll likely never read again. The Kindle is now available on the iPhone. And so we have come full circle. Always back to Steve Jobs and Apple.

No one solves problems better than Jobs. He solves problems we didn't know we had. My iPhone has become my Kindle, my iPod, my camera, my address book, my GPS, my radio, my Yellow Pages, my video recorder, movie player and television. Oh, and FaceTime—brilliant.

So, what's your problem?

The Ultimate CEO Pilot

On January 15, 2009, Chesley Sullenberger (Sully) was a pilot in command of an Airbus A320 from New York's LaGuardia Airport to Charlotte/Douglas International Airport in Charlotte, North Carolina. Shortly after taking off, Sullenberger reported to air traffic control that the plane had hit a large flock of birds, disabling both engines. Several passengers saw the left engine on fire.

Sullenberger discussed with air traffic control the possibilities of either returning to LaGuardia or attempting to land at the Teterboro Airport in New Jersey. However, Sully quickly decided that neither option was feasible, and determined ditching in the Hudson River was the only option for everyone's survival.

He told the passengers to "brace for impact," then piloted the plane to a smooth landing in the river. All passengers and crew members survived. He later said, "It was very quiet as we worked my co-pilot and me. We were a team. But to have zero thrust coming out of those engines was shocking—the silence." Sully checked the passenger cabin twice to make sure everyone had evacuated before retrieving the plane's maintenance logbook and being the last to evacuate the aircraft.

Sullenberger learned to fly when he was 16. He graduated from the US Air Force Academy in 1969 as "top flier." He served as a fighter pilot before becoming a commercial pilot. To say he loved to fly is an understatement. He became a master at aeronautics.

After the landing on the Hudson he said the following in a 60 Minutes interview: "One way of looking at this might be that for 42 years, I've been making small, regular deposits in this bank of experience: education and training. And on January 15th the balance was sufficient so that I could make a very large withdrawal."

A Thrown Situation

Let's say you're driving down a dark winding road, it's raining hard, your windshield wipers are on turbo speed. Suddenly a deer jumps out of the woods right in front of you. You are in a thrown situation. You have to react. You must react. You don't have the time or the resources to evaluate all options and consequences. So you rely on your values—your ideology.

Admittedly, if you put a dozen people in this same situation you'll get a variety of reactions. Some will brace for impact and strike the deer. Others will swerve into the unknown to avoid killing an animal. Neither reaction is the best. It's what you believe and value.

In this economy we are in a thrown situation. Situations that we're not familiar with are literally thrown in front of us. This is when people make bad decisions. Consider the Toyota gas pedal incident.

Toyota brands have been synonymous with quality and reliability. Not a flashy brand, but if you want a car that retains resale value and is rarely in the shop, Toyota is the one to pick. It is also the first commercially successful hybrid vehicle on the market. Toyota could do no wrong.

The lawsuits started to surface, and it appears that Aikido Toyoda, the CEO and pilot, may have known about the potential pedal problem in 2008, but did not issue a recall until

2010. He was in a thrown situation. So why did he throw out his stellar reputation by ignoring it and trying to cover it up? It was apparently for profit.

Does Toyota value safety, quality, reliability and reputation or the bottom line? Many now think Toyoda succumbed to the latter and have doubts about the once-trustworthy auto manufacturing company. Toyota sales will tell the tale.

How you react in a thrown situation is critical to your long-term reputation.

In 1982, a 12-year-old Elk Grove, Illinois girl died after taking a capsule of Extra Strength Tylenol. Six more people died shortly thereafter. The tampered bottles came from different factories, and the seven deaths had all occurred in the Chicago area, so the possibility of sabotage during production was ruled out. Instead, it was believed that the culprits entered supermarkets and drug stores and pilfered packages, laced them with cyanide and then replaced the bottles.

Johnson & Johnson halted Tylenol production and advertising immediately and just 5 days later issued a national wide recall of Tylenol products: an estimated 31 million bottles, with a retail value of over $100 million.

The media gave Johnson & Johnson much positive coverage for its handling of the crisis. For example, an article in the *Washington Post* said, "Johnson & Johnson has effectively demonstrated how a major business ought to handle a disaster."

Johnson & Johnson said it was an easy decision. It fell back on its values. On their website you can see a sample of the company's credo with the introduction:

"The values that guide our decision making are spelled out in Our Credo. Put simply, Our Credo challenges us to put the needs and well-being of the people we serve *first*.

Our Credo is more than just a moral compass. We believe it's a recipe for business success. The fact that Johnson & Johnson is one of only a handful of companies that have flourished through more than a century of change is proof of that."

People not profits, is, of course, the credo of the credit union movement. We have to constantly ask if we are true to the credo.

Data Rules the World

Financial institutions have more information about their customers than any other industry in the United States. Think about it for a minute. A credit union typically has the following information about a member: Social Security number, income, age, address, phone number, number and amounts of savings and loan accounts, as well as credit score.

This data affluence is a competitive advantage for those organizations that take advantage of it, but most do not for a variety of reasons. Information is closeted in many companies while organizational silos are proving hard to tear down. Information is still power.

Marketing strategies are often based on data that is developed by looking backward in time to past behaviors and by placing consumers into tidy demographic units. Demographics have value, but they also have their limits; they fail to provide insight into the consumer's frequency of usage, their channel or product preferences.

In the past decade data has become one of the raw materials for American business, equally as important as labor and capital. The turning point for the data evolution had its origins in Y2K, when companies built new technology architectures to guard against the meltdown that never came.

For companies that are using data effectively, financial relationships and predictive analytics make assumptions of potential buyers and their future behaviors. Predictive analytics uses a number of techniques from statistics and data mining that analyze bits of information to make predictions about future behavior. Credit scoring is an example of a predictive analytics application, which takes a member's credit history, loan application and other data to predict future loan payments made in a timely manner.

Organizations now have potent technologies to interact directly with customers as well as to collect and mine information that allows them to tailor products and services to the customer's needs based on that data, according to the authors of "Rethinking Marketing," published in the *Harvard Business Review*.[i]

The difference between a traditional company and a customer-focused one, according to the authors, is an organization that is organized to push products and brands, or in the worse case scenario, stalking marketing, whereby a customer-focused company serves customer needs.

The authors point to American Express as an example of a company that actively monitors customer behavior and responds to changes by offering different products. The organization uses data analysis and algorithms to establish the next product to offer according to the consumer's activities and behaviors. The purchase of an upper class ticket on a Gold Card, for instance, may trigger an offer to upgrade to a Platinum Card. This offer goes to a small number of customers, but it is highly effective and profitable.

American Express also uses its relationships between customers and local merchants to create value. The company may use

i Rust, Roland, Moorman, Christine, and Bhalla, Gaurav, îRethinking Marketing,î Harvard Business Review, January-February, 2010.

demographic information, customer purchases and credit reports to determine that a customer has moved to a new home. Given this life event, American Express offers membership rewards on purchases from merchants in the local network in home furnishings.

The authors offer four marketing strategies in the new environment:

- *First, shift from marketing products to cultivating customers*; focusing more on customer profitability rather than product profitability. Retailers have long offered loss leaders to strengthen customer relationships while taking a hit on certain products.
- *Second, pay less attention to current sales and more to the long-term value of the customer*. The concept of the lifetime value of the relationship, of course, is relevant to credit unions. This changes the focus from short-term profits to long-term health of the organization.
- *Third, change focus from brand equity to customer equity,* which is the sum of the lifetime value of the customer. Credit unions want lifetime members who value the organization as their primary financial institution.
- *Finally, companies should pay more value to customer equity share*, which can be measured by the company's customer base divided by the total value of the customers in the market. The authors maintain that customer equity share is a measure of the firm's long-term competiveness in relation to profitability.

The successful companies of the future will reinvent marketing departments as customer-focused departments with a new leader, a chief customer officer, write the authors. There are 300 chief customer officers currently, up from 30 in 2003.

Member Relationship Management

Member Relationship Management, also known as Customer Relationship Management, is a valued tool to manage data. It's the foundation for a sales and service culture, enabled by technology that puts the member first in all interactions. MRM is not a technology fix, but rather a cultural and a people transformation.[ii]

With a well-run MRM system, all of a member's interactions—products and services, problems and their resolutions—with the credit union can be found on one screen or one or two clicks away. To the member, the process is undetectable, but the effect is striking. The member need only tell their story once, rather than repeating it each time a call is made to the credit union.

The representative then keys in the information about the member. The financial institution that masters this task will have members and customers aplenty, as repetition over the phone or at the teller window is highly annoying to the consumer. Needless repetition moves the consumer to ask, "If they can't remember my story, what else will they forget?"

All data is then found in the same place and can be accessed by any employee. This helps to ensure that the data remains accurate and reliable. In the past some employees would keep information in places that can't be found by other employees. With MRM, there is no longer a need to call Irma in accounting to find where she keeps a piece of information needed to complete a transaction.

ii *"CRM Strategies," by Jim Jerving, a white paper by CUNA's Operations, Sales & Service Council, December 2010.*

This brings to mind a publisher once responsible for a book publishing unit. The mysteries of the publisher's accounting department were kept in one accountant's head. When that person went on vacation or was ill, the publisher was in serious trouble. And when that accountant finally retired, the troubles really piled up.

A membership relationship management system can also be used to enable marketing to keep track of which campaigns are used for specific member segments. Mass mailings of the latest and greatest car loan offer to every member are expensive and, worse, irritating to those uninterested in buying a car. And dinner time calls made to members can and should be allowed to fade away.

Some credit unions are investigating real-time optimization technologies to better combine historical customer information with real-time behavioral data to react more quickly to member changes. If a member, for instance, makes a large withdrawal or deposit, the information is given to the frontline employee who contacts that member within a day with a relevant product or service.

Transforming an organization to a sales and service culture is the decisive challenge in developing a member relationship management system. Employees accustomed to working in an order-taking environment will need to make dramatic changes in their work styles. Some employees are unable to make the change. But credit unions are competing with other financial institutions and retailers, where sales and service cultures as well as customer relationship management systems are firmly in place.

The financial services industry's digital evolution will continue briskly in the near future. A fully functioning MRM system allows credit unions to tap into the data wealth that they already possess and develop marketing campaigns that provide a competitive advantage in an unforgiving industry that keeps getting smaller.

As the authors of the *Harvard Business Review* article conclude, "Most companies use customer relationship management and other technologies to get a handle on customers, but no amount of technology can really improve the situation as long as companies are set up to market products rather than cultivate customers."[iii]

Agreed. We need to stop stalking and start developing and cultivating relationships with our members.

SIDEBAR
Advertising Dies a Slow Death

What is the 2020 Vision of Marketing? Advertising will be dead.

That's why so many marketers today are not willing to concede that it will happen. They are, quite frankly, in denial. They are following the five stages of accepting death.

Denial. This can't be happening to me.

There's no way I'm going to do anything different. So what if we aren't getting the response we wanted, I'll blame the economy. Television and Radio ads will always be around. And direct mail—c'mon. How will our members know what products we offer if we don't tell them?

Anger. This isn't fair!

I won awards for these marketing efforts! I have trophies in my office to prove that my radio, television and newspaper ads were winners! If we stopped all of that marketing, we'd go under.

Bargaining. I'll do anything to keep things as they were— just for a little while longer. Just until I retire.

---

iii *Rust, Roland, Moorman, Christine, and Bhalla, Gaurav, "Rethinking Marketing," Harvard Business Review, January-February, 2010.*

Well, I can't just STOP all marketing. What would I do? I have to keep to my marketing calendar, but I'll dabble in social media. When I have time…

Depression. I'm so sad, why bother with anything?

Pepsi and FedEx didn't advertise on Super Bowl Sunday. Could it be true? Is this a warning shot?

Acceptance. I'm going to be okay.

I'm open to exploring this thing called Social Media. I don't know exactly what it all means, but I'm willing to go there.. I accept that things are changing—rapidly—and I need new tools in my toolbox.

The Marketer as Co-Pilot:

In 2000 we were celebrating the non-event that distracted us for over a year—the impending doom that was to be the Y2K crisis. Remember that? It was marketing's warning shot and we ignored it. Marketing was classified as a "non-essential function." Should the computer catastrophe pan out, there was to be no marketing effort or expense in the aftermath.

So relieved were we that our computers came up on New Year's Day that we just kept right on with our quarterly advertising campaigns promoting bland products with puns and photos of happy people. No one wanted to concede the well-deserved label—excess baggage—that was slapped on our department during the drills for doomsday.

We're in the midst of the greatest economic crisis since the Depression. Marketing budgets are getting hit and marketers are getting laid off. Was it true? Have we made ourselves non-essential in a time of crisis?

Marketing *is more important* than ever, but *advertising* is dying a slow and painful death. In the next 10 years, the following trends will become reality:

1. Local radio broadcasts funded by advertisers will go silent.

- Northwestern University doesn't offer a single degree in radio anymore because, as the dean of that school says, "Students are not interested in radio."
- Since the Telecommunications Act of 1996 was put into effect, the consolidation of the industry has created a homogeneous, far less creative industry. Small markets are laying off employees and getting rid of most, if not all, of their local programming.
- The growth of Internet radio. It's already being made available as a factory installed option in many automobiles. If you have an iPhone with Pandora and an auxiliary jack in your car, chances are you never listen to radio advertisements.
- Wall Street has already seen the writing on the wall. That is why today there is no pure play radio stock that is valued above a dollar.

2. Passive advertiser-funded bundled cable ads will no longer be tolerated.

Simply put, the middle man that is cable television will be cut out. Television commercials will become a minor player. That model is outdated, ineffective, expensive and annoying.

- Hulu, Netflix, iTunes and YouTube has created an uprising in consumer television habits.
- The current cable system is being challenged with pay-per-view via micro payments and subscriptions.
- Broadcast TV is now digital, which means that cable companies are constrained as to how much they could charge for network TV in an a-la-carte world.

3. Newspapers—printed and dropped on your front porch—will become a novelty and specialty item.

- Rupert Murdoch, chairman of News Corporation, believes the future of newspapers is digital. In May 2009 he said, "Instead of an analog paper printed on paper you may get it on a panel which would be mobile, which will receive the whole newspaper over the air (and) be updated every hour or two."
- One year later the iPad is launched with iPad apps from all the major newspapers. Subscribers pay for content, not advertising.

4. The Post Office will be privatized and people will have the option to no longer receive mail—direct mail—at their place of residence.

Okay, this might be a bit of a stretch, but the numbers are pretty scary.

- The Post Office recently announced its plans to eliminate Saturday delivery to stave off bankruptcy. Mail volume has dropped from a peak of 213 billion pieces in 2006 to 177 billion in 2009. Quite simply, there is much less mail to be delivered thanks to e-mail, cell phones and texting, yet the cost to deliver mail continues to rise.
- In Australia there is a "Do not call, do not mail" option for all residents. By simply putting a sticker on your mailbox, the post will not deliver direct mail.
- It is estimated that 100 million trees are harvested to produce junk mail annually. As more and more companies push for green policies, direct mail will be questioned.

What does this mean if you are a marketer today? It's time we get some new tools in our toolbox to remain relevant.

The discipline of marketing is changing from advertising and product pushing to conversational marketing, a practice that involves engagement and interaction, a two-way communication rather than a one-way flow of information.

As Joseph Jaffe points out in his new book *Flip the Funnel*, "Marketing is not a campaign, it is a commitment."

The 2020 vision of marketing is that of a co-pilot. Someone with the right skills to fly the plane if need be. This person also has to clearly understand the vision or destination. They have to know how to use a compass and submit a flight plan.

As we mentioned earlier, most marketers today could not step in for the pilot/CEO. They're not even on the plane. They are on the ground in an office scanning through pages and pages of stock art of shiny, happy people, coordinating with printers and mail houses to generate their latest pun-undrum of a direct mail piece. Spray and pray. Focusing on the "me too" product instead of the differentiator.

So how do we get the marketer from the cubical to the cockpit? It begins with the understanding of brand. Yes, the "B" word.

Marketing is the custodian of a company's brand or reputation. Every company has a brand. When we hear someone declare that they are going through a re-branding, we can't help but think—good luck. You cannot change your reputation overnight. And a new logo and website will create a reaction, but what you do every day dictates your real position in the mind of the consumer.

Chapter Five

The Pilot and Co-Pilot Chart Their Course

Warning: This exercise is not for the faint of heart. It requires brutal honesty, some soul searching and possibly arm wrestling.

In previous chapters we've talked about some of the greatest business leaders—pilots of their organizations—in recent history. We found that they all had one thing in common—a sense of direction. Their true north. In times of crisis, they relied on that moral compass to see them through, and it works.

So, let's talk about your values. As we stated earlier, in a thrown situation your values cannot be faked. Your values enable reflex reactions.

According to *businessdictionary.com*, values are defined as:

Important or enduring beliefs or ideals shared by the members of a culture about what is good or desirable and what is not. Values exert major influence on the behavior of an individual and serve as broad guidelines in all situations.

That last line is critical. Values exert major influence on behavior. In other words, in business, what you value is what you're willing to measure, manage and most importantly reward.

This is not what you have to measure, but what you obsess over. What drives you? What's your definition of success?

Many of the financial institutions I've worked with over the years claim to value service. It feels like the right thing to do after all, they are IN the service business. Few of them actually measure, manage and/or reward service. They are merely paying it lip service. When confronted with this fact, many have defended their position by saying that service is hard to measure. If you're serious about service, Chapter 6, the net promoter score, shows you how to measure it. Figure B applies the Ripple Effect and applies it to values.

Figure B
The Ripple Effect Applied to Values

"The Ripple Effect"

values = what you measure, manage & reward

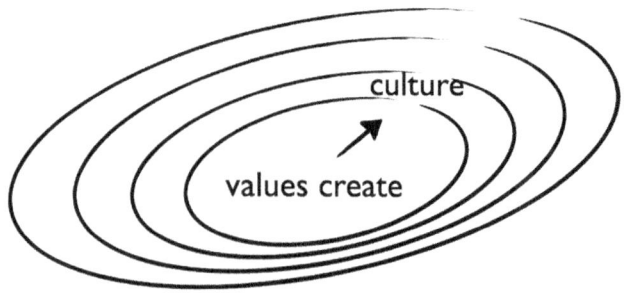

If you want to determine what you really value in your organization, you must turn to our painful exercise number one:

Ideally the marketing person should bring in an outside facilitator to direct this process because it gets a little personal. The atmosphere in which you conduct this session is *über* important.

Picture a nice sunny room, not the dingy room in the basement with the hissing fluorescent lights, and some good coffee. Now make sure you have those Post-it® brand of flip charts—best invention since wheels on luggage—and some juicy felt pens. Now you're ready to do that soul searching. To begin uncovering what the CEO truly values, begin with these simple questions:

1. What numbers do you look at every day? Every week? Monthly? Yearly?
2. Is there an incentive program in place? What drives the incentive?
3. How do people get raises? Merit? Goals? Likeability?
4. What do you celebrate at work?
5. Why do people get terminated?
6. When new people come on board, is there a probation period? What do they have to wait for? Are certain cultural things withheld?
7. How often do you meet? With leadership? Staff?
8. In your meetings, is there an agenda? What's the format generally like? What's the purpose?
9. What kind of behavior would you say you reward?
10. What behavior gets punished?

That's a good start. Now you should be able to begin to see how the culture of your organization was developed. The real learning is in detecting patterns. If you're trying to build a culture of service and many believe this is their differentiator—but the majority of your rewards are geared to sales—service takes a back seat. You can talk about it all you like, you can hang banners in the lunch room and market, but if you don't measure, manage and reward the effort daily you'll never be a service leader.

That's measuring your culture from the inside out. Now to truly determine your reputation, the Net Promoter Score will tell you what you're known for and you can see from the outside in.

Achieving alignment with what you want and what you have is vital.

Your values create your culture.

Creating the Brand Filter

As we mentioned in part one, successful companies have one thing in common—a succinct brand filter. And this filter is practiced like a religion. It's not a suggestion; it's the company's moral compass. Johnson & Johnson saved lives first, with the net result of saving their reputation by staying true to its filter in a time of crisis.

The filter has to reflect what the CEO values. What they measure, manage and reward. What does your CEO lose sleep over? Service? Sales? Margin? Profit? Employee morale?

Your brand filter should not be viewed as a slogan or a tag line. In fact, it's something that your members should never see—rather they should feel it. Steve Jobs and "user experience" is felt the first time you turn on an iPod, iPad or MacBook Pro.

Amazon.com's filter of "We make money when we help people make purchase decisions" is felt each time you log on and read real reviews for the products it sells.

Your brand filter needs to reflect a promise to work from your values.

Once you've determined your filter—what you want to be known for—you need to use it to question everything. Go back to your goals, your incentive programs, your products and services. Do they pass easily through your filter? If you've been honest, you probably have to change some things. Give some things up. Maybe discontinue bad profits. Or pay more attention to employees.

Chapter Six

Net Promoter Score®[iv]: The Marketer's Dashboard

Many credit unions believe that service is their differentiator. They also believe that they have a reputation for great service. And yet when you ask how often they measure it, "annually" or "not at all" is often the answer. In the past, there haven't been easy or accurate ways to gauge service levels. Satisfaction surveys didn't cut it because they asked the wrong questions.

Banking is an errand. Just like going to the post office, the grocery store or the gas station. Members don't get to go to the credit union unless they have to. They are satisfied if they can get in, get out, and nobody gets hurt. Banking for most people is not a joyous occasion; it's a chore and for some it's an anxiety ridden journey.

The Net Promoter Score isn't a survey; it's a discipline, like accounting. It's not a fad. Fred Reichheld's goal is to have NPS™ become a General Accepted Account Practice (GAAP). His twenty-year study of loyalty economics shows a direct correlation between NPS and the bottom-line.

We recommend the groundbreaking book, *The Ultimate Question*, by Fred Reichheld to gain an understanding of the discipline of NPS.

On the surface the NPS survey is quite simple. We'll give you the basics in this chapter and whet your appetite for more.

---

iv *Satmetrix and the Satmetrix logo are registered trademarks of Satmetrix Systems, Inc. Net Promoter, NPS, and Net Promoter Score are trademarks of Satmetrix Systems, Inc., Bain & Company, and Fred Reichheld.*

We truly believe that this measure is the missing link between marketing's efforts and the bottom line of the organization. If the marketer's job is that of custodian of the brand, they need a dashboard that tells them how the brand is doing. NPS is a predictor of future growth, not a rear-view look at what's happened, like so many other accounting measures.

As we've emphasized throughout this book: *corporations don't have values, people do.* What you value is what you measure, manage and reward. If you've not been measuring service as frequently as ROA, you don't value it.

NSP asks the ultimate question: "How likely are you to recommend the credit union to a friend, family member or co-worker?" The answers—on a scale of 0 to 10—will get you a score. But the *real* value is in the follow-up question. Why did you answer the way you did? Figure C applies the Ripple Effect to NPS.

Figure C
The Ripple Effect Applied to NPS

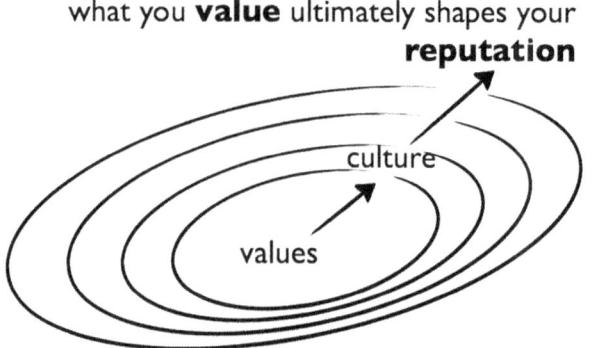

"The Ripple Effect and NPS"

what you **value** ultimately shapes your **reputation**

culture

values

that is what NPS measures.

Trustworthy Data

Are you willing to make business decisions based on the data?

We make business decisions when reliable data is available. Key ratios such as loan-to-share, delinquency and operating-expense-to-assets guide our decision making. The accounting methods we use are steeped in manufacturing. We manufacture loans and deposits and access devices—and so does our competition. Our real product is service. We need to begin measuring that as rigorously as we do the bottom line.

The Right Questions

The more questions you ask in a survey, the lower the response rate. This is known as survey fatigue.

Response rate is as important as the overall score. If you get an 85% NPS, but if only 50 members responded, it's not reliable.

"You can't grow a business unless you treat people so well that they come back and bring their friends," said Fred Reichheld. The right questions, according to Reichheld's and Brooks' research, are simply:

"How likely are you to recommend the credit union to a family member, friend or co-worker?" The follow-up questions need to probe why the survey taker would—or would not—recommend the credit union. As a general rule, no more than five questions should be asked due to survey fatigue.

The Right Members

This is called the "value of the voice." As a not-for-profit financial cooperative, it's important that we hear from and give value to the right members. Most credit unions lack a target audience. Instead, they have designated a field of membership that is often a territory or a list of Select Employee Groups.

Consider the 80/20 rule. About 20 percent of the members of any credit union account for 80 percent of the business; these are your profitable members. These members have value. You need to hear their voices. It doesn't mean you don't hear from other members, but you do need to make sure that your top 20 percent can recommend you. And you need to know why, or why not.

The Right Time

There are two types of surveys you'll want to do—transactional and relationship. Relationship surveys measure experience periodically over the lifetime of a member. Transactional measures experience following a specific event. Right after a transaction a member should get the survey. These surveys can't be anonymous. We need to know exactly who filled out the survey.

Closing the Loop

Every time you send out a survey, you are basically launching a campaign against yourself. You're asking your members if you are worth their time. That's why response rate is as important as the score. Since the point of NPS is to measure word-of-mouth it's important that through your survey process you generate as much positive word-of-mouth as possible. You can do that by responding to all detractors in your transactional surveys. By closing the loop with your members—within 48 hours—you're sure to generate positive word-of-mouth that the credit union is serious about service.

The following transactional surveys should be conducted quarterly, and should include:

- Your branches: (the errand)
- Online
- Phone
- New member
- New product (loan, CDs)

By surveying the right members, with the right questions at the right time, you will be able to see patterns. The data will become reliable. Business decisions can now be made. You now have actionable data. You've moved from anecdotal to quantifiable.

A Discipline like Accounting

Every month you measure and manage loan quality, member activity as it pertains to deposits, withdrawals and fees. All this tells us is traffic flow. How many members did what and got what. This measuring does not tell you the likelihood that you will get that business in the future.

Business is built on relationships, even though accounting doesn't make that clear. Of course members want good economic value, but they want more. Loyalty is about the emotional side. But both sides—economic and emotional—are essential.

Companies with higher customer retention rates have higher profitability. Loyalty creates lots of cost and revenue advantages throughout the value chain that accumulate into a big impact on growth and profits.

Reichheld calls this a "growth engine" and NPS measures the health of your engine.

Bad Profits

The scores in segments and touch points should be able to guide your decision-making, budgeting and prioritize your projects. It will also give you a tool to avoid bad profits.

Bad profits are those that are made at the expense of a member relationship. Fee income is becoming more and more necessary as margins continue to tighten. Weighing the income against the drop in score will help guide you in your decision making.

"Our members just love courtesy pay!" Rather than relying on anecdotal evidence, quantify that love with the ultimate question. Are they just willing to pay for it? Or do they love it so much they would recommend it to their friends?

Actionable Data

So, let's say you know that your new member experience could be better. You are getting quarterly survey responses from your new members, and now it's time to really look at the responses and make some changes.

Using a tool called the Member Corridor, you can easily identify those points of pain, where, if it goes wrong, you get detractors, and points of Wow, and if you deliver the unexpected consistently you breed promoters.

Your goal is to change the perceptions of the credit union. By examining a specific point of contact with a member, a "touch point," you can differentiate your credit union by creating an experience that your competition cannot easily copy.

Using the Member Corridor to Create Wow

The customer corridor was actually developed by Virgin Media. It was looking for a program that would engage and align employees. It wanted something that was easy to understand and that would reliably improve the customer experience.

Virgin Media's customer corridor was developed by a cross-functional team to describe, in detail, the journey through the customer's eyes. Not the back office. It was important to list each and every touch point along the way, beginning with awareness and marketing, all the way to repurchase.

In the NPS Certification course offered by Satmetrix, students used their experience of flying to the event to illustrate the basic use of this tool.

For example, the awareness, or beginning, was rather complex. How did the participants decide which airline to fly? Price? Reputation? Loyalty? Web presence? This first touch point was critical to purchase. But then there are such things as checking luggage, the boarding process, in flight entertainment—or lack of—and the ever-important landing of the plane. There are many steps in between that we didn't mention.

But here's the big "ah-ha" moment for the class. After agreeing on the many touch points for the customer, each student was asked individually to rank their top two in terms of importance. Not surprisingly, the majority said "arriving on time, alive and with my luggage." The airline has, for the most part, complete control of these issues. Out of 40 students engaged in this activity, all but one received their luggage and only a handful was delayed. The majority got what they wanted.

So, the burning question—are they now promoters? Overwhelmingly not. But why? Very few airline experiences are anything to write home about. Expectations are at an all time low. Service for the most part is poor. Bad profits abound. Airlines are on the lowest rung of the Profit Zone—commodity with no cost advantage. They are too big to fail. They're like the old monopoly AT&T—we don't have to care.

Except for Southwest Airlines. They consistently post the highest Net Promoter Score in their industry and, not surprisingly, the highest profits. Figure D presents the Member Corridor, which encompasses the entire member experience capturing data at every touch point.

Figure D
The Member Corridor

The member corridor

The member corridor encompasses the entire experience capturing data at every touch point

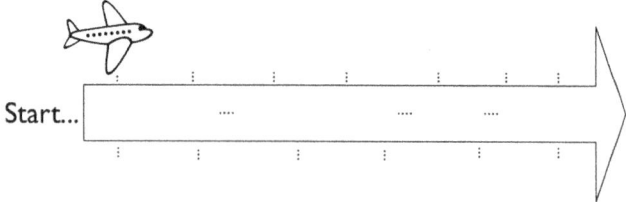

Start...

The Internal Net Promoter Score

If you are really serious about embracing the truth about your culture, you should consider an Internal Net Promoter Score. We recommend these 3 questions:

1. On a scale of 0—10, how likely would you recommend the credit union as an employer?
2. Why did you answer the way you did?

3. What would you recommend the CEO:
    a. Stop doing?
    b. Keep doing?
    c. Start doing?

If you are not ready to hear the answers to these questions, avoid the internal survey. The worst thing that can happen— you ask, you hear, you get angry and do nothing or worse yet, retaliate.

It is not recommended that you conduct this survey yourself. Or use an online tool to capture data. Unlike the member survey, this one has to be anonymous or you will not get reliable data. We have facilitated this process the old fashioned way. We think it's important that all employees meet at the same time. It doesn't have to be in the same location, but it's important that they are not given the opportunity to collaborate. They should not know the survey is coming. Your monthly staff/branch meetings are the perfect venue.

Each person is given the survey and ample time to complete it. Then they are given an envelope to seal themselves. These envelopes are dropped into a FedEx package that is addressed to the third party, in this case the authors, and sealed in front of everyone.

It might seem a bit extreme but we've found this always yields the brutal truth and online, like Survey Monkey, type tools do not.

The most important part of this survey? Your reaction. Like all surveys you are looking for patterns. Think about it. Let's say you have seven branches and an administrative building. You conduct this survey as we've suggested and you find out that 50 percent of your staff thinks a new product launch was ill-conceived and is creating member detractors. That is reliable data—and that actually happened to us.

The management team thought this member reward program was great. They trained and marketed it. Employees did complain, but management blamed accounting and marketing for its lack of acceptance. Turns out the product was inherently flawed. All the marketing and training in the world couldn't change the fact that instead of rewarding members, as the product name implied, it was punitive. This data combined with member data resulted in an overnight killing of the product. Not a single member complained and the staff had faith in management again.

For companies serious about culture, the internal and external NPS programs are a requirement.

Chapter Seven

This is not about Social Media

When we first started writing the 2020 Vision of Marketing we naturally asked, "So how much of it should be about social media?" We came to this conclusion. None of it and all of it. Social media is not Facebook, Twitter, or the new tool *du jour* is by the time you read this. It's a fundamental shift in the way we communicate. It does not fix problems. It cannot make you hip and cool if you're not hip and cool. We feel that every organization needs to make the shift from marketing that includes pushing, stalking and screaming to first observing. The tools provided to you, we hope, will do that.

Observe what you truly value by being honest with what you measure and manage. If it's a service culture you're trying to create, and then have the guts to measure it using the Net Promoter Score.

We also believe that as a marketer, your job is first and foremost to create a brand that is worth talking about. Generation Y will market for you using whatever social media tools they love at the moment to guide people to you. It's not unlike the way marketing started in credit unions. We served a group of people with a common bond. We solved a problem for them. We were willing to do things for them that banks would not. And we knew them by name, listened to their stories and took chances. They in turn would go back to the office, the warehouse or the classroom and tell their co-workers how great their credit union was.

That was social media without a cell phone or computer. It's not being on Facebook it's being the best. The smartest thing you can do is join the conversation. Let go of controlling it. Invite participation. Stop stalking and start talking.

Just for fun:

To Blog or not to Blog--Our recommended tool for "marketing"

Everyone wants to blog. No one wants to write one.
—Jeffry Pilcher

We love to blog. Why? Because it's a place that we can just dump our thoughts. It's a Petri dish of ideas and total randomness.

We'll see something in our travels and think, "Oh man, we have to blog about that!" It's like hearing a song and thinking that it has to be on the next party mix tape.

It's easy because we're interested in the art and science of marketing. We're not trying to sell stuff, or be clever, or fake being excited about something to sell—like the features and benefits of a free checking account. And that's why a lot of people say they want a blog—but never do it. They don't know what to write about, so they say, "I don't have time."

We are all granted 24 hours each day to do with as we please. No one can buy more time; no one is punished with less. It's God's little equalizing gift to us all. What you choose to do with those 24 hours speaks volumes about your priorities and your passion.

Most of our posts are written in one take. Our grammar and sentence structure would sometimes prompt Sister Rose Dolores to pull out her ruler and hit our collective knuckles.

It's our little corner of the world, and written like the spoken word. And that's what makes it interesting.

We are both honored and humbled to have readers. It changes the way we feel when sitting down to write. Like now, for instance. We realize someone might be reading this—besides us. Thanks for stopping by. Our hope is not to disappoint.

So if you want a blog, and you fail to write a blog, because you lack time, you won't make the time. If you're spending hours each week sitting in mind-numbing meetings, then racing back to your desk to wade through stacks of mundane e-mails, feeling no progress whatsoever, well, we can't remedy that, it's basic time management.

The following blog was written by Denise Wymore in her blog, the 2020 Vision of Marketing, **http://denisewymore. wordpress.com/page/3/**

It was written on May 12, 2010 and was featured on the Freshly Pressed page of Wordpress Freshly Pressed is the best of 340,223 bloggers, 453,149 new posts, 259,206 comments & 80,382,190 words on May 12, 2010. It received a record 56 comments. It was a big day for Denise. It also marked her two-year blogging anniversary.

Enjoy.

Why Do We Have Meetings?

Heard this morning from someone I admire:

"Meetings for the most part are completely unproductive, mind numbing and do nothing to foster teamwork."

As a consultant, I am the maker of meetings. When I come to town, we're going to meet. I see it in their eyes when I enter the board room. *Oh gawd, what is SHE going to make us do?*

I pride myself on having productive meetings. Here are a few things I've found that help to turn your meeting from a time waster to a treasure.

1. Don't have a meeting in the basement. You cannot be creative with fluorescent light. In fact studies have shown that artificial light sucks about 1.5 pounds of your soul from your body each hour.

2. Have an agenda. This sounds like a no-brainer but many people come to meetings because they are "on the calendar" not because they have a purpose or a goal.

3. Calculate the value of the attendees time when the meeting starts and the value of the outcome. Once the time expense has exceeded the value, someone is instructed to signal the meeting's end with a blow horn.

4. Cut your meeting time in half. Seldom do meetings end early. This always puzzles me. They almost always end on time – because people have to get to their next meeting. Hmmmm......

5. Good coffee with real cream. Powdered cream says "We hate you and don't value your opinion."

6. Ban all Crackberries, iPhones, Droids, distractions. If the meeting is not important enough for you to turn off your email – you don't need to have the meeting.

I'm just sayin'
Now, I gotta go. I have a meeting at 7:30.

PART TWO

A FOCUS ON PURPOSE

How to Build a Culture of Service

There are a number of books on service: *Knock Your Socks Off, Raving Fans,* and *Service America.* Books that take a psychological approach like *Why This Horse Won't Drink.* And of course the marketing classics like *One-to-One Marketing.* But it really comes down to one individual:

The CEO. The Chief. The Leader.

If the CEO does not truly value service; if he or she does not require good service to ooze from every pore of the organization; if they are not willing to measure it and manage it and hold people accountable for it—you can not and will not be known for and benefit from a service culture.

This is the point of the entire book. You need to focus on purpose.

If you are a commodity—and financial services is a commodity—and you do not obsess over service, social media will overpower you. That's our vision for the year 2020.

Here's the brutal fact about social media. It is the largest referral campaign in human history, and it's only going to get bigger. It's not a fad. It's not an anomaly. Social media is a megaphone with global reach that has magnified what humans have been doing forever—telling their friends about their experiences. You can't hide from it. You can't control it. And you better not ignore it.

We bet some of you reading this are thinking:

It's dangerous and I will not allow my company to engage in it. Our IT department has seen to that. We will not let employees access their social media fan pages at work. We have strict controls in place on the Internet so that our front line staff cannot access anything but our home page.

The following chapters will tie all of the tools together to do one thing. Create an organization that truly differentiates itself with service. Now I know what you're thinking. Impossible. Or, we know we have great service. The reality is that most of us have service that is just okay.

But here's the bottom line. We live in a service economy. America doesn't make anything anymore. We shifted from an industrial society to an information society over 30 years ago.

If that doesn't convince you, perhaps this will. For the last 20 years interest rates have been declining to historic lows. Rates have nowhere to go but up. It's easy to market loan products in a declining rate environment. But go ask your marketer this question: "What font are you going to use when your auto loan rates go up by 50 basis points? What shiny happy people stock art are you going to purchase to entice a 20 year-old to come to you for their first new car loan?"

You ready to get serious about service? About reputation? Let's do this!

Killing your Culture

It's easier to kill off an organism than it is to change it. This is why brand new businesses in the social media world can grow so big so fast. They didn't have to change the way they do business. Instead they have the benefit of looking at the antiquated models that are limping along and simply go in the opposite direction.

Okay, it's not as simple as that, but consider Facebook and the phone book. Betty White appeared on the May 8, 2010 episode of Saturday Night Live because of a Facebook campaign. Producer Lorne Michaels succumbed to the pressure and invited the 88-year-old Ms. White to be the oldest host by far in SNL history. Her opening monologue was historic. She thanked the nice people on Facebook for their support but admitted she had no idea what Facebook was. She went on to admit that once she logged into Facebook she thought it was a tremendous waste of time. In her day they had a "phone book" but, she admits, she wouldn't waste an afternoon on it.

It's a funny anecdote but really a powerful symbol of the social media world. Could it have been possible for the Yellow Pages brand to have launched the Facebook model and been successful? Let's say Mark Zuckerberg's dad owned Yellow Pages. If he were to have built an exact copy of The Facebook architecture and targeted those households that still listed themselves in the phone book, would it have worked? Would those people post their profiles? Friend each other? Not likely—and here's why.

1. **The target audience**. Facebook was an extension of the year book model. It originally invited only Harvard students to join. A common bond. A tightly knit community. The phone book is just a list of people who live in a region. No common bond.

2. **The phone book's reputation**. Two things come to mind that are hard to shake. Number one, that it was commonly used to prop up toddlers at the dinner table. Number two, Steve Martin's line in the movie, The Jerk, "The new phone books are here, the new phone books are here—I'm somebody."

3. **This is totally a stereotype**—but the kind of people who still list their names in the phone book are a) old and not popular and b) old and still have a land line.

4. **The logo and old tagline**. *Let your fingers do the walking through the Yellow Pages*. It would be hard to morph that into something relevant and compelling. I guess

you could say "Let your fingers do the clicking on Facebook."

5. **Environmentalists have trashed Yellow Pages reputation** recently by highlighting the fact that 20 years after the mass introduction of the Internet, Yellow Pages continues to kill trees and print books that stack up in mail rooms around the nation. Stop it already.

So you're the Yellow Pages and you need to morph into something cool like Facebook. Where to begin?

We believe you can create a loyal following for any product by simply focusing on service. And we have proof that it can be done.

A Wake Up Call: Service Differentiates and Creates Profits

If you feel that service no longer can be a differentiator—and there are many out there who feel this way—then you probably fall into one of two categories: market researchers still clinging to the last vestiges of their discipline or accountants. Managing a culture of service is harder than sitting in a boardroom pouring over financials and surveys and piles of trends, graphs and charts. It requires you to get engaged. Get out of the corner office and set an example.

Ron Shevlin, author of the now retired blog *Marketing ROI* and his new blog *Marketing Tea Party* had this to say about an *Adweek* daily briefing entitled *Is Customer Service the New Marketing?[iv]* After one of the blurbs in a recent Adweek/IQ Daily Briefing email posed the question: Is customer service the new marketing? According to the email:

"Nowadays things are changing. Customers looking for products simply type them into Google. Assuming you can get customers this way, the hard work then begins: keeping them. That's why, according to Andy Ridlinger, customer service is now serving the role of marketing.

"Companies need to start treating customer service as an investment rather than an expense. The necessary 'white glove' level of service required to create raving fans is more expensive in the short-term, but in the long term you not only spend less supporting current customers," he writes. "Their free word-of-mouth marketing will help you add more customers."

This is a misguided idea.

If customer service is now serving the role of marketing, then who's planning and executing campaigns? Who's determining the allocation of marketing dollars across channels and programs? Who's figuring out which customers the firm wants as "raving fans" in the first place?

The customer service department, which has a 40 to 60% annual turnover among personnel in some organizations? The department that is increasingly outsourced to some offshore service provider?

The notion that "customer service is the new marketing" is the epitome of wishful thinking. "Let's just be nice to customers and they'll tell all their friends and we'll make money hand over fist."

Our answer to Mr. Shevlin's idea is quite simply, "Yes." Thank you. If you are nice to your customers, they will tell their friends—on Facebook—and you'll make money.

What he fails to understand is that we are a service economy. To be successful long term it's going to become imperative that you get the *service thing* down.

We have undergone a fundamental shift since the conclusion of World War II, at which time service industries accounted for 10% of non-farm employment, compared with 38% manufacturing. In 2005 workers who provide services (111.5 million) outnumbered workers who produced goods (22.1 million) by a ratio of five-to-one.[iv]

The Definition of Service: An act of assistance.

The Definition of Good Service: Exceeding the low expectations of consumers.

The Definition of WOW Service: Choreographing, compensating and communicating the bottom line value.

We have little or no control over the quality of the product we deliver. But we have ultimate control over the way we deliver—the act of assistance. Whether you're in the healthcare industry, hospitality, transportation, financial services, government, even utilities, you are providing a service.

Thanks to Net Promoter Score—explained in chapter six—more companies are able to quantify the value of good service. Or as Fred Reichheld, the author of the Net Promoter Score says, "You can't grow a business unless you treat people so well that they'll come back and bring their friends."

Social media is making sure of that. Before the invention of the Internet, marketers were in control of the message. Consumers were social creatures but in a cocoon that was network television with four channels and the local newspaper thrown on your porch each morning and AM/FM radio trapped in your car on your morning commute.

The early goal of marketing was to make you believe you didn't have options. Jingles were psychologically proven to embed themselves in your brain so when you went to the store where you did in fact have options somehow your subconscious would take over and your hand would reach for the Campbell's soup can. Your entire world was local and with limited options.

The Internet has given us choices. FedEx and UPS have given us unprecedented access. PayPal has given us peace of mind. Anyone can deliver the same product you can, but how you deliver it, service it, follow-up with it that's where the real money is.

JC Penney announced they were discontinuing their catalog. The Penneys catalog, like Sears was originally distributed to rural communities, that still exist today. These areas consist of small towns with no malls, no clothing stores, no way to buy appliances or toys or tires. The information super highway came in the form of the US Postal Service. The postman was the Internet.

How many of you were devastated by the news that the Penneys catalog was history? How many of you thought JC Penneys was gone? I know we did. Over the years Penneys and Sears competed on the catalog frontier. And how did they compete? Price? Service? Convenience? Somewhat. It became increasingly more difficult for them to differentiate. So began the "selection" or "one-stop-shop" game.

A mistake made by thousands of businesses every day. When sales are down, add services. Expand your offering. Add products and services that you know nothing about. In other words, let's try to be all things to all people.

That's when Sears and Penneys became unhinged. Instead of focusing on their core discipline—Craftsman and Kenmore quality—Sears partnered up with Super Models to get into the designer clothing space. Remember Cheryl Tiegs announcing her new line of Sears apparel?

Sears was founded in 1886. They had the "first to market" advantage for decades. But the Internet and social media changed everything. I'm sure there was research that showed that Cheryl Tiegs popularity would catapult the brand into the stratosphere by simply marketing her image. But it's service that wins the race.

You know the end of this story. K-Mart and their Jaclyn Smith line bought out the Sears brand and is now on the verge of bankruptcy.

Service—Pronounced "Serve Us!"

Why don't more businesses commit to being service leaders? Because it's difficult. Traditional marketing was easy. It's not effective anymore, but it's still pretty simple.

Creating and sustaining a culture of consistent, reliable and twitter worthy wow is hard.

But you're committed; otherwise you wouldn't still be reading this book.

As we mentioned earlier it begins at the top. And not just in the way of the emperor announcing from the balcony to the minions below that you are a service organization.

"Now go forth and serve."

Nope. You have to be a Carl.

The story of Carl and Les Schwab Tires.

The following is a personal experience written by Denise Wymore

Years ago, when I was living paycheck to paycheck as many service workers do, I found I had a flat tire when I was leaving my office. Luckily I had one of those cans of magic goo that will temporarily pump it up. But a friend of mine told me about this magic place called Les Schwab Tires that would fix your flat for free. I had that much money so I drove over.

Wasn't sure what time they closed but when I pulled in the driveway, before I could even get out of my car this guy came running up to my door. Now, my first reaction, since I did not live in a great area at the time, was "Oh No! Carjacking." Until I focused on his nicely pressed uniform with the Les Schwab logo embroidered on it.

"Welcome to Les Schwab!" he exclaimed opening up my door with flourish. What can we do for you today?" I explained my situation, he escorted me to the waiting room apologizing that they had a few people ahead of me but there's fresh coffee and a popcorn machine and good magazines to enjoy while I waited.

A note about the popcorn. This is choreographing wow. Popcorn is one of those snacks that you don't have to be in the mood for, even have to be hungry, but as soon as you smell it, you have to have it.

And, popcorn permeates and dominates a room. Popcorn on. Brilliant.

So I'm sitting there with the rest of the afterwork brood munching on popcorn, catching up on the Hollywood gossip in the trashy magazines they provided when the phone rang. Out walks Carl. He's the manager; it said so on his nice shirt. He answers the phone. He explains that they are already closed and there are several people ahead of her—she's still welcome to come in tonight or first thing in the morning and they will fix her flat lickity split. He even used that phrase *lickity split*. She decided to come in anyway.

She was greeted with all the fan fare of the customers on time; she enjoyed the popcorn and magazines. Carl was obsessed with service as his differentiator.

When my car was done they called my name, I wanted to pay by this time but they said "No, Ms. Wymore, fixing your flat tire is our gift to you. We just hope the next time you need new tires you'll think of us."

And with that I was gone. And you know what? I've told that story to hundreds of people at conferences; this was well before social media. If I were to blog about it today it would likely reach thousands of people.

Somewhere along the way the accounting department at Les Schwab figured out that by performing this one service for free it would result in increased sales. Loyalty economics is what Fred Reichheld would call that. This act of service is marketing. The word-of-mouth was free.

When I needed new tires? You got it—I went to Les Schwab. They are not the cheapest in town, but they provide the best service and only stock quality brands.

We did some research on this company. And here's what we found.

Les Schwab Tire Company began in 1952 when Les Schwab bought a small Rubber Welders tire store in Prineville, Oregon, where the company is currently headquartered. It is the leading tire retailer in the United States with more than 400 centers all over the Western part of the country. The company is famous for providing sudden services, warranties in writing and convenient credits. Les Schwab Tire Centers are engaged in community activities concerned with youth and families.

I also read that employees share in the profits of Les Schwab, and that Les is always mystery shopping his outlets.

Here's another interesting, marketing technique. Before getting into tires Les was a cattle rancher and apparently continued to own cattle. Each year he has a "free beef" promotion with a set of new tires. Weird? Yes. Differentiator? You bet.

Les Schwab did three things well:

- **Choreographed the wow**. The store I went to was in downtown Portland, Oregon. The dreary cold wet rainy weird capital of the world (and my home town). Let's put it this way—you don't want to be outside most of the time. And yet they require employees to run out in the elements and greet each and every customer.

The popcorn. Brilliant choreography. And in between tire rotations it's someone's job to keep it popping and coffee brewing.

Carl. Probably the biggest piece of choreography is that Carl, the manager, is engaged and constantly setting the example. He does not hide in the back room pouring over financials and reading trade magazines. You would not even suspect he was the manager were it not for his embroidered title on the shirt he proudly wears.

- **Compensated the wow**. I had heard that all employees are stock holders. Their service is rewarded monetarily by sharing in the profits of the company.
- **Communicated the value**. We can only imagine that they have some way of measuring the "free" services against the repeat business it yields. This is important to help the front line employees believe that what they are doing matters.

Les Schwab Eulogy and Epilogue:

On May 18, 2007 Mr. Schwab died on his ranch in Prineville, Oregon at the age of 89. In 1986 he wrote his autobiography, *Les Schwab, Pride in Performance, Keep it Going.*

I remember people speculating what would happen to the Les Schwab empire after he passed. He was, after all, the driving force behind the culture. Remember, corporations don't have values, people do.

Sadly Les' children both passed before him. One of cancer and one in an automobile accident so there was no one to carry on his legacy. Here's what I found today when I googled Les Schwab:

Les Schwab use to be what everyone looked to as the best example of customer service. Everyone I know went to Les for anything they provided. Be it brakes, shocks, struts, wheel alignment, tires you name it and asked if they would do tune ups etc.

So where did it all change? Everyone I know now avoids Les like the plague. Each and every one with a recent experience said they will not return. I personally got the scare about breaks, shocks, struts and front end. The car was "judged unsafe to drive" by one of their technician/salesman. I knew I needed tires so that was not a surprise. As for the rest, I went to another shop and was told Les flat out lied. I had 20,000 plus on most of the items I could not live without. They outright cracked up at Les' insistence that I had to have brake calipers. Nothing wrong with them.

May Les rest in peace.

Choreographing the Wow

There is no better example of choreographing wow than a Cirque du Soleil performance. If you've never been—you must go. It's hard to describe. They really created their own category of entertainment. It's not a circus—no animals at all—it's not a play. It's sort of a musical, but that shouldn't scare anyone away. It's a visual orgy of color, movement, and impossible choreography. Wikipedia calls it a dramatic mix of circus arts and street entertainment.

Here's an example of one move that is going on in the background while dancers are falling from the sky on red silk scarves only to stop inches from the stage. Somehow they built in trampolines in certain sections of the stage floor. Now picture a dancer tumbling in and then jumping on what looks like the floor only to catapult them up and diving head first through the third story window of an old warehouse. What? The precision, timing and agility of that one move is impressive and inspiring.

And yet you never hear of anyone dying, or falling or getting hurt. How can that be? Practice, practice, practice.

If you want to be a service leader you need to think like Cirque du Soleil. They have several different shows now ranging from tributes to Michael Jackson and the Beatles to kind of naked—Zumanity in Las Vegas—to the traditional O and Ka. It begins with the theme. Think of the story you want to tell.

Think of what you want your members to say about you. What do you want to be known for? And the answer can't be "great service." The secret to cracking this barrier is in choreographing the wow.

What follows is a story of two companies working together that get it:

Groupon and the Saffron Tiger--Planning for Success.

Meet the Fastest Growing Company Ever.[iv]

At least Mark Zuckerberg wrote a few lines of computer code at Harvard before he left to launch Facebook. Now Andrew Mason, a relaxed and lanky 29-year-old music major from Northwestern, has managed to build the fastest-growing company in Web history. Groupon represents what the dotcom boom was supposed to be all about: huge sales, easy profits and solid connection between bricks-and-mortar retailers and online consumers.

Groupon, a name that blends "group" and "coupon," presents an online audience with deep discounts on a product or service.

Act now, says the pitch: You have only so many hours before this offer expires. That's a familiar come-on, but it's coupled with a novel element: You get the deal only if a certain number of fellow citizens buy the same thing on the same day. It's a cents-off coupon married to a Friday-after-Thanksgiving shopping frenzy.

What's in it for the vendor—which might be a museum, a yoga studio or an ice cream shop? Exposure. Since the resulting revenue is not only discounted but shared—typically, 50/50—with Groupon, the vendor may scarcely break even on the incremental sales. But it now has customers who might never have thought of patronizing the business. Groupon gets its offers in front of eyeballs by buying ad space through Facebook and via **word of mouth** from its 13 million subscribers.

There are several key points to this article. The vendor may scarcely break even on the incremental sales. But it now has customers who might never have thought of patronizing the business.

This equals a moment of truth for the company. It's show time. Did you practice?

The Saffron Tiger is a fairly new Indian Buffet restaurant in a half empty strip mall in Albuquerque, New Mexico. Within one mile you have a Wendy's, McDonald's, Chik-Fil-A, Subway and a dozen local sandwich shops and burrito stands. There are lots of options. Saffron Tiger has been compared to Panda Express. You can dine in, or take out and the food is prepared in bulk, you look at the dishes, point and bam—they are packaged for you, you pay, and next! We're familiar with the model. But one of their challenges and oddly their differentiator—it's Indian food.

The Groupon offering was $15.00 worth of food for $7.00. The innovative thing about Groupon is that it's not a coupon;

you commit to buying the offer first and then cash in the coupon. In other words, in order to print it out—you must pay the $7.00.

You have one year to use the Groupon, which is good because 478 people bought it in the 24 hours it was offered. It would be chaos of all 478 queued up that day. We were dying to try it so we waited a day—hoping it wouldn't be that crowded.

When we arrived, as feared, there was a line. The kitchen is open to the public's view, it smelled heavenly, the place was immaculate and the service—efficient and pleasant. As we approached the counter we were greeted with a beaming employee—not a frantic, overwhelmed, unprepared for success minion. We had been eyeing the Chicken Masala and as luck would have it a fresh tray was being placed in the buffet line as we were ordering. We noticed a few pieces of Naan in a tray and decided to add a side of this delicious bread. They made a point of telling us that if we don't mind waiting 3 minutes they will make us some fresh bread.

No problem. That's when we noticed the "free sauce bar" with to go cups with lids, which included yogurt sauce, mint sauce and some kind of dangerously hot red sauce. This kept us busy while our bread was being cooked.

As she was handing us our "to go" order and thanking us I asked her "Have you had a lot of Groupon traffic?" "Oh yes," she beamed. "We're very excited."

That is the correct answer. How often do you plan for and celebrate overwhelming success with lines out the door, hours of being slammed, cash register burning up days of continued profit?

It's sad to admit—but most companies don't. They hope to get by. In the financial services world, where we come from this is what typically happens when a decision is made to expand and open a new branch.

First, research is done to find the perfect location for expansion. Or, a board member drives by an empty lot while shopping one night and says "We should see how much that costs, we could build a branch there."

Then an architect is brought in that likely has a reputation for building the competitions' branches. What's the latest trend? Coffee bar? Children's theatre pit? We want one too. No differentiation.

Then marketing is brought in to pick out the backlit pictures of shiny happy people or the perfect colonial style home with the red door and sporty convertible to display. We'll also announce our grand opening with door knockers and a party. We'll have clowns and balloons and roast hot dogs in the parking lot. It'll be swell.

The branch staff? HR will hire some and train them at another branch. We'll probably move a seasoned person over to be the branch manager. Nothing new here.

Except that's where they would be wrong. You only get one chance at a first impression. Think of it as a first date. You want another date? You better bring your A game. And it begins with construction.

Here's how to create a wow experience with a new branch for an old business.

The target audience. Get intimate with the neighborhood. After all, the research shows that within a three mile radius is where you will get the most traffic. What's your story? Why does this neighborhood need yet another financial institution?

Let's say your target is the soccer mom. What does banking represent in her life? It's a necessary—and often, unpleasant—errand. What could it represent? A way to help teach her kids about financial responsibility.

Like the Saffron Tiger, the menu must have the staples—the Indian cuisine lovers would expect, Naan, Masala, chickpeas. Where they chose to differentiate is with the buffet style and open kitchen. The target audience: the busy working professional. It must be fast and fresh. It's more expensive than lunch at Wendy's or McDonald's. They don't have a dollar menu. No one wants to eat cheap Indian food.

Too often marketers get hung up on the menu. Whenever we see a sign outside of a bank or credit union touting their "Free Checking" offering it's like a sign outside of a grocery store declaring "We Have Food." It's not why people go there. Free checking, is ubiquitous. But you need it on your menu.

So let's go back to the soccer mom, our target audience. Narrow and focused. What's our cause? What should be our brand filter? What can we do for these moms that no one else is doing and more importantly is not likely to copy?

How about helping them raise their kids financially? We can't count on the schools to do it anymore and we know that many parents could use the education themselves.

Now we have our target and our filter.

- Busy working soccer moms = target
- Helping them raise their kids financially = culture filter, or how we will differentiate.

We must use that filter so the brand message oozes from every pore of the organization. The performance must be wow. And the performance must be rehearsed.

Marketing as Choreography

Step One: Building the Stage and Creating Hype

Too often we see the missed opportunity in opening a new branch, the construction site. Most marketers will get a vinyl banner printed up and drape it over the cyclone fence with the phrase "Future home of AB Credit Union."

When something new is being built in your hood—you watch intently for the announcement. Will it be an adult video store? A Starbucks? A new restaurant? Oh, it's another bank or credit union and you drive on.

But the anticipation of those three to six months of construction is priceless. Imagine changing the banner every month? Not revealing the name of the company until two weeks before the grand opening? Here's an opportunity to capitalize on the captive audience by creating buzz. And no trite marketing messages like "Coming Soon—Your Community Financial Partner."

How about something cryptic and targeted only to your soccer moms. Like the standings of the grade school soccer teams? Or partnering with a local sports store and advertising a sale on soccer cleats?

How about launching the dirtiest soccer mom van contest? Drive them to a website to enter and announce the winner at the grand opening and surprise them with a new soccer mom van?

Now you have your marketing hook. You should be building up excitement and anticipation for the Grand Opening. Now you need to plan for overwhelming success.

We recommend that you rehearse the chaos. Don't train your new staff at an old branch. They must be able to easily navigate their stage for the performance to be flawless. Spend at least a week playing out different scenarios before opening night.

The goal is overwhelming success? Right? What does that look like? How many new accounts will you open? How many of those honestly represent a soccer mom moving her checking from your competitor? There is no bigger pain in the ass than that.

How will you endear yourself to her? Can you be her human switch kit? Get permission and access to her old account so you can take on the arduous task of canceling automatic withdrawals from one place to yours?

Now some of you may be overwhelmed by this and find all kinds of reasons why it can't happen. And if you feel that way, put the book down and light a candle and pray you will live to work another day.

If you're not overwhelmed but energized by these ideas, remember, you have to do what is right and relevant for your marketplace. The soccer mom is just an example; it's a metaphor for how to narrowly target.

We've had some fun with the open house. We wowed them on the first date. Now we need to seal the deal and get them to recommend your credit union to friends.

Remember our filter? Helping parents raise their kids financially. What does that mean? Let's look at the development of a child's financial awareness.

From ages one to five kids are on a steep learning curve. They learn an entire language, all of their basic motor skills are honed, and then there's the basic concepts of time, and math and reading and writing. This is why we have kid's' clubs with kangaroos and dinosaurs and puppies. Save a buck, get a pup. Keep it simple and fun, they are going through a lot in these years.

But then we start earning an allowance and understanding that the ATM doesn't just give us money, we have to earn it first. Here's where you can help the parent teach a kid to save for stuff. It can be as simple as "What are you saving for?" and allowing the parent to go online with their child and name a savings account. Every kid wants a Wii these days. Let them designate a Wii savings account.

Kids grow up fast these days, so by age 10 and 11 they want their first plastic card. What a great opportunity to introduce a prepaid VISA card as a convenience for uploading their allowance. Now you can introduce the concept of a monthly statement and even itemizing expenses. At an early age you can identify Starbucks dependency or Slushee.

By age 15 they are gearing up to drive. It's inevitable and a stressful time for any parent. In addition to having driver's education resources, you could offer seminars at the branch that features a hot car, the kind that would make any teenager salivate. Have a mechanic take them through the basics of that car, what could go wrong, basic maintenance like oil changes. Then have an insurance agent come in and show how they set their premiums. What happens to your monthly premium if you get a speeding ticket? Then have them calculate the monthly cost of driving. Today gas can range from $3.00 to $4.00 a gallon. The average car gets 22 miles per gallon.

By age 18 they may want their own place and their own car. If the parent is willing and able to co-sign for the child we suggest this. In the spirit of helping the parent raise their kids financially you present them with a contract. Optional, of course, and approved by the parent before the transaction. This contract will do two things; first, it explains to the parent that by co-signing they are putting their credit score at risk. Should the child default, and they do not pay, they will be required to pay with a blemish on their credit history. Secondly it acts as a contract between the parent and the child.

The child needs to understand the credit score and the fact that they do not have one yet. The parent is putting up their score to benefit the child. The child needs to make monthly payments on time to build a good score. If the child fails to, the parent can select to be active in the repossession process. Something like, "I have the right to meet you at the mall in front of your friends and ask for the keys to your car leaving you no choice but to take the bus home."

This is not a legal, binding contract, but rather a tool for the parent to opt to use to educate their child. The parent will see you as a partner in the process.

These are just a few ideas, but we hope you get the idea. By narrowly targeting an audience and offering something unique that your competition is not willing or able to copy you will create word of mouth. Social media tools will take care of the marketing for you.

Your members that are not soccer moms? They still get the regular menu items. Nobody's going home hungry. There's still free checking, reasonable rates on auto loans, access to credit with VISA, and home equity lines of credit.

To ensure overwhelming success you must chose to be great at a few things. Not mediocre at all things.

Compensating for WOW

It's time for our obligatory Nordstrom story. What business book about great service in the last 30 years left out Nordstrom? Very few. So here goes.

As told by Denise Wymore.

I dated a well put together guy in my early twenties. He was the perfect man. He loved to shop, was a wonderful cook, had an immaculate apartment and best of all was a snappy dresser. This guy loved Nordstrom. He loved their no hassle return policy, their amazing sales team, the lighting, the music, everything Nordstrom quality.

He was hosting a Christmas party at his place and took me to the mall because he just had to have a red sweater vest. They didn't have a v-neck sweater in his size at Nordy's. They called the other two stores in the Portland area and they were out as well. Seems red sweaters are quite popular in December. Who knew?

But in the spirit of WOW this clerk was not done. He asked my friend when he needed the sweater. We had a couple of days before the party. He got his name and address and said he'd see what he could find. This clever salesman that gets paid on commission decided to go to their competitor, Meier & Frank—now owned by the conglomerate that is Macy's...grrrrr. They had a Jantzen brand sweater, red v-neck in his size. When he called to make sure this would suffice he also asked if he'd be home that evening. And here's where choreographing the wow makes sense. The employee delivered the sweater to his home.

Word-of-mouth? Repeat business? You bet. That's the 2020 Vision of Marketing - to focus on the purpose. It's no secret that Nordstrom employees can make six figure salaries in retail. Nordstrom has never been nor will ever be cheap. But service is legendary.

How do you compensate for service in the banking world? No one does it better than Umpqua Bank. They measure service rigorously, by employee, by branch. They also pay for sales. But, there's only a consequence if your service numbers are down. You don't give legendary service at Umpqua, you will be fired. If you never make a sale, who cares? That's a bonus. But if you are not serving, you're not an Umpquanian.

Now to be clear, the top service people also have high sales. But the compensation is geared to service. The consequence for not delivering—is focused only on service. What gets measured gets managed and gets done. Too often financial institutions put in sales quotas and marketing campaigns that shamelessly push the product of the month with no regard to the actual need. This is frustrating for both the employee and the customer or member.

Until recently, measuring service levels has been difficult. In our opinion, Net Promoter Score is the simplest and easiest way, to measure and compensate for service. The relationship score—the random sample of all accounts on a quarterly basis—should be included in company wide profit sharing. After all, this is a true measure of the health of the reputation and everyone, from accounting, to HR to marketing to the front line contributes to that reputation. Remember the Ripple Effect way back on page 13?

The transaction score can focus on the products and services that you want to be known for. In the case of the soccer mom, you would consider the following events to trigger a survey:

- The new account - first date.
- The pre-loaded VISA card set-up
- The co-signed car loan closing

This score can accurately pinpoint the employee's performance as well as identify any root causes of detractors. This is where the discipline of NPS comes into play.

There must be consequences for employees not achieving wow levels of service by creating promoters. Put another way, you may have to fire employees who are not of the servant mentality.

Communicating the Value of Service

Fred Reichheld calls his 25 plus years of study loyalty economics. He set out to prove that treating people well and having them come back and refer contributes mightily to the bottom line. Quite simply his research goes back to the golden rule.

Too many executives consider that model to be too touchy feely. But the reality is, it's difficult to measure and manage. It's easier to stay in the corner office and make decisions based on the bottom line, rather than any kind of strategic initiative that will help you stand out in the marketplace.

This is perhaps the most difficult and the most necessary step in building a wow service culture: Communicating the value of service.

Companies like Disney, USAA, Southwest Airlines and Zappos.com have all shared their secrets to culture creation. In each case it begins with the interview and orientation process.

USAA, which serves only military and their families makes all new hires walk a mile in their shoes. They eat Meals Ready to Eat during training, and have to experience the weight and reality of combat boots, packs and weapons. They practice empathy like a religion. The result is one of the highest Net Promoter Scores in the world and consistent profits.

The Southwest Airlines interview process is intense and includes the candidate having to tell a joke and be in on one. Pilots, mechanics and flight attendants experience the same process. You either have a sense of humor, or you don't. It's a key component of their culture.

Zappos.com also has every employee spend two weeks on the phone with customers. That interaction is the soul of their culture and unlike most companies they do not measure number of calls. They do not care how long an employee is on the phone with a customer; it's all about the experience. The measure NPS daily and can boast a 91% score along with 68% repeat business on any given day.

Southwest Airlines founder Herb Kelleher will fire a customer before they will fire an employee. He will not allow customers to bully their employees. Southwest Airlines also had the guts to allow cameras to film their product—the flying experience—in the show Airplane on the A & E Network. It ran for 70 episodes. Would you allow cameras to film your moments of truth?

And now let's discuss empowerment. When we were an industrial economy there was no such thing as empowerment. It's something management had to learn. In manufacturing you are told what to do, how to do it but rarely why. Training was specific. It was up to management to put the right people on the line and up to training to teach them to pull the right levers at the right time. If you didn't, we would step in and retrain. If you still didn't, you were replaced, or in the case of union contracts, moved on down the line.

Pull. Weld. Stamp. Seal. Push. Done.

In a service economy we are dealing with human beings who are fickle, unpredictable and elusive.

In a service organization like a credit union or bank you do have to teach people how to do things. For example, how to book a loan on the computer. You also have to tell them when to do certain things. Like when Truth in Savings rules kick in and need to be compliant with the law. Most importantly you need to train people in a service organization why they have to do thing things they do. By having the background, they can be empowered to make decisions on their own, educated decisions. That's the key.

Too often financial organizations try to reduce their risk by giving power to only a few—the gatekeepers of decision making. You often see this on the teller line and in the loan department, which are the two riskiest areas of operation. Instead of allowing and encouraging a teller to get to know the member, they get to know the check they are trying to deposit, specifically the amount. If it's over X dollars, it goes to the gate keeper. The service experience begins to suffer. We are no longer serving the member; we are serving the bottom line.

Show us a check cashing policy that never takes a bad check and we'll show you one that doesn't take checks. We are in the risk business. We should budget for it. Mitigate it, yes, but try to eliminate it? Impossible.

It's like the dressing room policy of allowing no more than six garments per fitting room. This is to hopefully eliminate the shoplifter. Less than 1% of retail customers shop lift and yet 99% are inconvenienced, demeaned and fed up with this rule. And this has not eliminated shoplifting.

We asked a head teller at a large credit union why they have built a system of such tight controls. Her response was shocking. She cited two reasons. The first was high turnover in the teller row. The head teller had the benefit of years of experience in spotting bad checks. Makes sense. The second was the caliber of employee. She went on to say "Besides, we don't trust most of these tellers to make a good decision. They don't care."

It was quite obvious to us that the real problem was with the culture, not the tellers. The first obvious question is: "Why is the turnover so high?" And the second, "Why do you hire idiots?"

This is one of those horrible things that is usually answered "Because we've always done it that way." We've always paid tellers a barely livable wage, which forces them to either get out or move up as soon as possible creating a constant influx of new bodies barely trained to fill the void." Brilliant. So the front facing position—the most important position—is poorly staffed and barely trained.

As Alyce Cornyn Selby, author of *Whatever Happened to Team Work* would say,

"Stop Doing What Doesn't Work!"

There, we said it. If you want to be known for good service you have to have the guts to pay your staff for it and train them adequately.

How do you train people to give good service? We have two answers. The first one is, you can't. Some people are raised with the servant mentality and some people are not. If you truly value service, you have to be trained on the functions of the job, why things are done a certain way and then get out of their way. Empower them. Let them serve.

The other answer is lead by example. Be a Carl Schwab. Be Mr. Beazely, from Denise's first book and her first boss. Each year on Thanksgiving morning, Mr. Beazely would invite all of his servers to come to the restaurant to be served by him. He preached service, at a Fish-n-Chips restaurant to high school girls dressed in wench costumes. Quite simply,

Mr. Beazely would say, "We were put on this earth to serve one another. Whether you're filling up the tartar sauce cups or frying halibut, if you are serving someone, you are doing work that matters."

That's right. Service matters. Good service makes money.

If we empower people, mistakes will be made!

Even the gatekeepers make mistakes. Like we've said before, we are in the risk business and people intent on committing fraud are always coming up with new and innovative ways to do it. You can't possibly keep up.

A truly empowered service culture will stand by employee decisions. As long as the employee has a rational reason for doing what they did, based on the information they had then the decision must be supported. Not punished. We see these wounded warriors every day. Glazed over, robot-like movements, never going to make a mistake again. Service drones with the life beaten out of them.

Denise made a colossal mistake at the peak of her career with a very large credit union. In the spirit of innovation and differentiation her team built a new website using Macromedia Flash in 1997. It was brand new technology but her target audience, the high tech employee should embrace it.

What her team did not count on, was that Home Banking should've been called Office Banking. The site went live on Monday morning, right about the time members were arriving at their offices, booting up their computers and logging into home banking. They were met at the website door with a Flash message that they must download the key. Their network Nazis would not allow this. Consequently, their innovation brought their organization to its knees. Angry members lit up the call center, corporate intranets screamed our failure and stupidity. We had no choice but to yank down the baby and put up the old site.

Denise was sure she was going to be fired. But her boss understood what happened. There was really no way of knowing that a high tech company would not embrace this technology. Instead of being reprimanded her boss had this to say.

"You tried something new, it didn't work. People who never make mistakes, in my opinion, aren't doing anything worthwhile."

From that day forward she learned to take educated risks. Most of the time it paid off, but empowering her to try was the secret to success.

Acknowledgements

From Denise Wymore

Thank you to Mary Beth King for editing this book and for generously donating the cover photograph.

To the credit union movement for being my family for the last 30 years - sometimes dysfunctional and crazy (like a real family) but always there for me.

To my writing partner Jim Jerving who put up with my stops and starts and three moves while creating this book.

To the ladies at Pop's in Gearhart, Oregon for your lemon scones, coffee and morning chats. You were the only people I talked to during my week-long writing retreat, and you beautifully kick started my day. Oh, and the lemon scones will seriously change your life.

A big thank you to all my blog readers and social media guides (Tim, Matt, Brent, Gene, James Robert, Roger, Glenn) for keeping me writing every day.

And to my partner Mark. Here's to many more years of traveling, hiking, laughing.

From Jim Jerving

Thanks to the women in my life, Beatrice, Sara and Julia Jerving, and Chris Martell.

Thanks to Denise Wymore, my writing partner for an enjoyable experience. And thanks to Mary Beth King for her great editing.